"Enter the magical world of colors and imagination with my coloring book for children, where every page is an invitation to explore and create!"

I am grateful to God for everything!! And I believe that the meaning of life is to give meaning to other lives and you are the meaning of my life!!

Jair Arandiba
2024

This Book Belongs to:

○—————————————————————————————○

Test Color Page

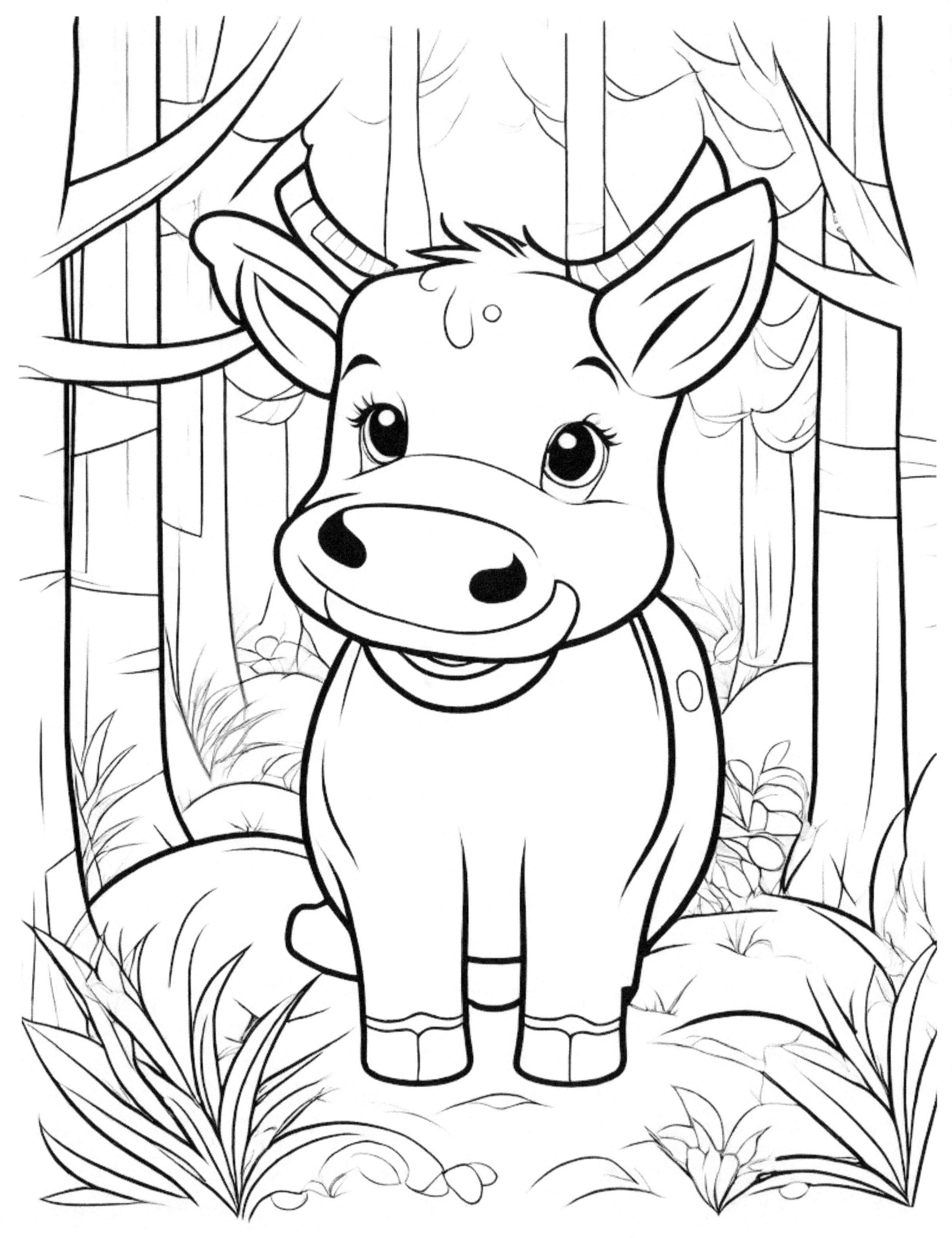

www.ingramcontent.com/pod-product-compliance
Lightning Source LLC
Chambersburg PA
CBHW081451250726
48662CB00009B/3028